THE ARAPAHO

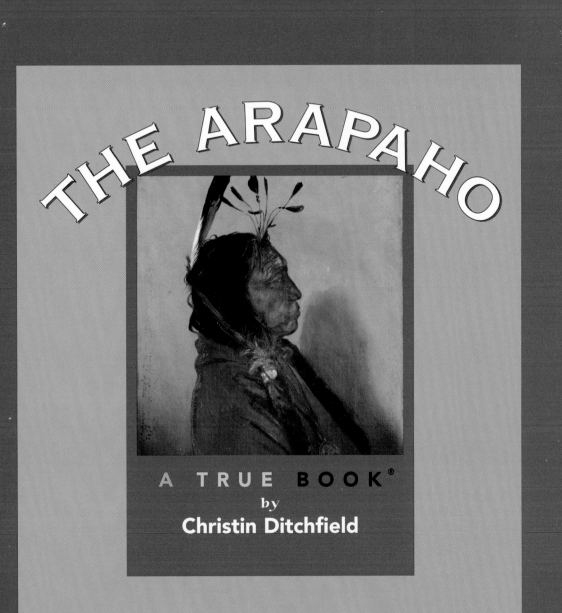

A TRUE BOOK®

by
Christin Ditchfield

Children's Press®
A Division of Scholastic Inc.

New York Toronto London Auckland Sydney
Mexico City New Delhi Hong Kong
Danbury, Connecticut

A scene from
an Arapaho Sun
Dance painted on
a muslin cloth

Content Consultant
Liz Sonneborn

*The photo on the
title page shows
Arapaho Chief
Black Coyote.*

Library of Congress Cataloging-in-Publication Data
Ditchfield, Christin.
   The Arapaho / by Christin Ditchfield.
      p. cm. — (A true book)
   Includes bibliographical references and index.
   ISBN 0-516-23642-3 (lib. bdg.)   0-516-25586-X (pbk.)
   1. Arapaho Indians—Social life and customs—Juvenile literature.
2. Arapaho Indians—History—Juvenile literature. I. Title. II. Series.
E99.A7D55 2005
978.004'97354—dc22   2004030518

CHILDREN'S PRESS, and A TRUE BOOK™, and associated logos are
trademarks and/or registered trademarks of Scholastic Library Publishing.
SCHOLASTIC and associated logos are trademarks and/or registered
trademarks of Scholastic Inc.

1 2 3 4 5 6 7 8 9 10 R 14 13 12 11 10 09 08 07 06 05

Contents

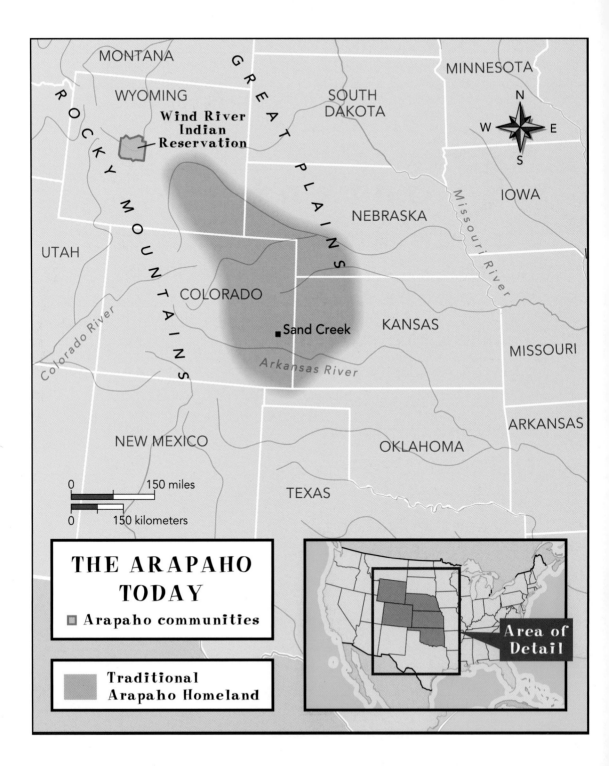

MONTANA

WYOMING

Wind River Indian Reservation

GREAT PLAINS

SOUTH DAKOTA

MINNESOTA

N
W E
S

ROCKY MOUNTAINS

IOWA

Missouri River

UTAH

NEBRASKA

Colorado River

COLORADO

■ Sand Creek

KANSAS

Arkansas River

MISSOURI

NEW MEXICO

OKLAHOMA

ARKANSAS

TEXAS

0   150 miles
0   150 kilometers

THE ARAPAHO TODAY

☐ **Arapaho communities**

Area of Detail

Traditional Arapaho Homeland

People of the Great Plains

American Indians have lived on the continent of North America for thousands of years. Many of them gathered around the Great Lakes. Known as the Algonquian people, they settled in parts of Minnesota, North Dakota, Michigan, and Canada. They raised their families in homes and villages that were part of large farming communities.

Over time, the Algonquian people began to **migrate** away from the area. They separated into different tribes. Each tribe developed its own **culture** and language. By the 1600s, these tribes had become "people of the plains." They did not live in one place. Instead, they traveled constantly across the Great Plains—through Wyoming, Colorado, Kansas, Oklahoma, Nebraska, and Montana.

The Wind River Mountains rise above the Shoshone National Forest in Wyoming. Today, many Arapaho and Shoshone live on the Wind River Reservation in Wyoming.

This Indian family, like many other Plains Indian families, traveled the Great Plains. Plains Indians traveled to follow buffalo herds and find other food sources.

They moved from place to place in search of food, good hunting, and warm weather.

One of these tribes became known as the Arapaho. This name probably comes from the Pawnee word *tirapihu*. This means "he buys or trades." The Arapaho called themselves *Inuna-ina* (*Hinóno'éno*), which means "our people." They were also known as the Sky People or Roaming People. Other Plains Indian tribes, such as the Cheyenne and the Sioux, called them Cloud Men.

A Nomadic Life

For more than 200 years, the Arapaho lived a **nomadic** life. They were highly skilled horsemen and expert buffalo hunters. They followed the herds across the Great Plains.

The Arapaho camped in cone-shaped tents called tepees. Tepees were made of

A group of tepees form an Arapaho camp near Fort Dodge, Kansas, in 1870.

buffalo skins stretched over long wooden poles. These tents could be put up or taken down quickly. This was impor- tant when the tribe needed to move on. Tepee walls were often decorated with paintings of great warriors and hunters. The tepees had very little furniture inside. The family slept on a wooden platform. A fire kept them warm.

From time to time, the Arapaho fought with enemy tribes. Sometimes they conducted raids to capture more horses. For the most part, however, they lived in peace with their neighbors. They

developed trading relationships with other tribes. The Arapaho exchanged buffalo skins and meat for vegetables such as corn and beans.

Arapaho men hunted buffalo, deer, and elk. The women gathered roots, berries, and herbs. These were used in soups, stews, and special teas.

The Arapaho made their clothing from animal skins, usually the skins of deer or elk. Men wore shirts and leggings, along with breechcloths (aprons with front and back flaps hanging from the waist). Women wore leggings and long dresses decorated with

Bear Woman and Freckle Face were two Arapaho women. This photograph of them taken in 1898 shows the traditional clothing worn by women of the tribe.

paint, beads, and porcupine quills. Both men and women wore shoes called moccasins. In the winter, they bundled up in buffalo skin robes.

Growing Up Arapaho

The Arapaho believed there were four stages in life: childhood, youth, adulthood, and old age. As members of the tribe passed from one stage to another, the community celebrated with special ceremonies and **rituals**.

When a new baby was born, older relatives would come and

A portrait of Arapaho George Shakspear shows the three piercings in his left ear. Arapaho children had their first ear piercings when they were between the ages of two and five.

pray for the baby's health and strength. Young children had their ears pierced when they were between the ages of two and five. This was not done so

THREE INDIAN DOLLS
Donated by Sholie Richards Brown

RAW-HIDE BAG
Arapahoe
Donated by Sholie Richards Brown

that they could wear jewelry, but to help them learn to handle pain. Little boys pretended to hunt like their fathers. They played war games, as well as hoops and

18

darts. Little girls played with tiny tepees and rawhide dolls.

As they grew older, boys and girls were separated. Girls spent time with older women in the tribe, preparing for the day when they would marry and have families of their own. Arapaho girls learned to cook, sew clothing, and build tepees. They often became skilled artists, designing beautiful patterns and pictures with beads and paint.

Boys entered military societies, which were groups organized according to age and skill level. They began in the Kit Fox Lodge. As they learned certain skills—and grew older—they were promoted to the next group. These included the Star, Tomahawk, Spear, Crazy, and Dog groups. There were eight stages in all. When a young man completed all eight stages, he was considered a full-fledged warrior.

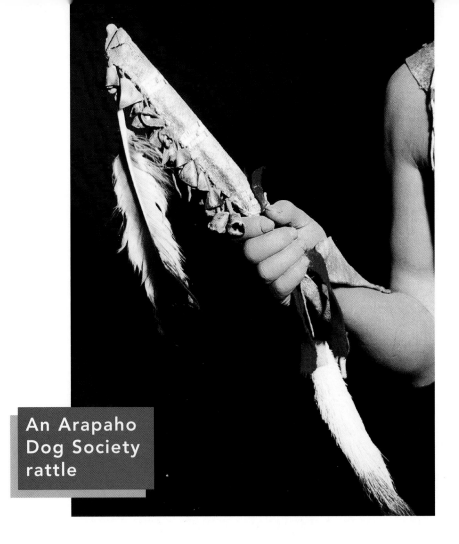

An Arapaho
Dog Society
rattle

This meant he had all the privi-
leges and responsibilities of an
adult member of the tribe.

Calling on the Creator

Tribal members shared a deep faith in the Creator God who made the world and the Arapaho people. They believed that he would give them health and happiness if they honored him.

Every year, the tribe gathered for the Sun Dance, their most

A group of Arapaho children and men on horseback pose near a Sun Dance camp in the late 1800s. The tribe gathered each year for this important ceremony.

important religious ceremony. To prepare for the Sun Dance, members often went without food or sleep for days. Then they sang and danced and performed **complex** rituals.

Some American Indian art is inspired by visions.

The Arapaho looked for spiritual guidance through visions and dreams. Sometimes a person would go out alone to hear what the Creator might say to him or her. This was called a vision quest.

Tribal members also kept their own medicine bundles. These were containers they filled with personal belongings and **sacred** objects that were thought to have supernatural powers.

To the Arapaho, the flat pipe was the most sacred object of all. This wooden tobacco pipe stretched almost 2 feet

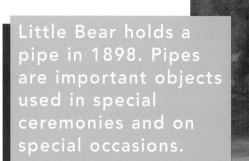

Little Bear holds a pipe in 1898. Pipes are important objects used in special ceremonies and on special occasions.

(0.6 meter) long. It was wrapped carefully in a bundle of animal skins. The flat pipe could be opened and smoked only on the most special occasions.

Black Bear and Little Raven

The Arapaho did not have many chiefs and leaders. Everyone in the tribe participated in making important decisions for the community. Still, some leaders played a very important role in Arapaho history.

Little Raven

Black Bear was a famous Northern Arapaho chief who bravely led his people into battle against the U.S. Army. This was after the Sand Creek Massacre of 1864.

Little Raven was a Southern Arapaho chief known for his wisdom and speaking skills. He helped negotiate treaties with the U.S. government on behalf of the Arapaho nation.

A Tribe Divided

In the 1800s, President Thomas Jefferson sent a group of explorers to scout out the land beyond the Mississippi River. He wanted them to see if they could find their way to the Pacific Ocean. These explorers discovered all the wonders of the American West.

Many pioneer families crossed the Great Plains in covered wagons.

Soon thousands of white **settlers** began moving across the Great Plains. Some built

Pioneer families travel the Oregon Trail through Wyoming on their way farther west.

their homes right in the middle of Arapaho lands. Others passed through the area on their way to Oregon and

California. The area could not support all these people. The wagon trains disturbed the migrating patterns of the buffalo. The natural environment was destroyed. Food became hard to find.

The Arapaho had to compete with other tribes for what was left of the land and its resources. They traded with settlers for guns, knives, and other weapons. Soon they had to trade for food and clothing.

By 1835, the Arapaho had split into two tribes. The Northern Arapaho moved into Wyoming, and the Southern Arapaho moved to Oklahoma. Unlike neighboring tribes, the Arapaho tried to keep peace with the settlers and avoid conflict. But sometimes they did get pulled into battle.

One of the saddest days in Arapaho history was in November 1864. A peaceful group of Southern Arapaho and Southern Cheyenne were

The attack on Arapaho and Cheyenne Indians at Sand Creek was a terrible day in American history. U.S. Army soldiers killed many innocent people in the massacre.

camped at Sand Creek in Colorado. The U.S. Army attacked them while they lay sleeping. Many American

Indians were killed, including women and children. This led to a six-month war between the Arapaho and the U.S. military.

As time went on, the Arapaho lost many members of their tribe to war, **famine**, and disease. They signed peace treaties and agreed to move onto reservations—land set aside for them by the U.S. government. The Northern Arapaho settled on the Wind River Reservation in Wyoming. They shared the

Arapaho and Cheyenne council members meet in Oklahoma in 1900.

land with the Shoshone. The Southern Arapaho settled in Oklahoma with the Cheyenne.

The Arapaho Today

Today, there are more than 6,000 Arapaho in the United States. Most of them still live on or near the reservations in Wyoming and Oklahoma.

In many ways, the Arapaho are just like other Americans. They wear the same clothes and drive the same cars.

Some Arapaho work as firefighters. This group of firefighters from the Cheyenne-Arapaho nation in Oklahoma assisted in looking for debris from the space shuttle Columbia disaster in 2003.

Quilt making and archery are just two traditional Arapaho skills. Many adults work to pass these skills down to the children of their tribe.

They live in houses and apart-
ment buildings. They operate
farms, breed cattle, and
run businesses.

At the same time, the
Arapaho try to preserve their
history and culture. They want
to pass on their traditions to
the next generation. One of
the biggest challenges for
the Arapaho people is finding
a way to preserve their
language. Only about 1,000
people know how to speak

Arapaho. The youngest of those people is forty-five years old! If younger people don't learn how to speak the language, one day it will completely disappear. Tribal members are working on programs for kindergarten and elementary school children. They want to help them learn the Arapaho language at school. That's how they hope to keep their language alive and well.

Rescuing a Dying Language

Dr. Stephen Greymorning is a **linguistic anthropologist**—a scientist who studies language and culture. As a member of the Arapaho tribe, he is concerned about the future of the Arapaho language. He looks for new ways to teach the language to the next generation.

In 1994, Dr. Greymorning came up with a great idea. He convinced the Walt Disney Company to produce an Arapaho version of the movie *Bambi.* This was the first time any Disney film had been translated into an American Indian language. Now Arapaho children can learn the language of their ancestors while watching a favorite movie.

Traditional dances are performed at annual festivals.

Each year, the Northern and Southern Arapaho gather together at festivals to sing the old songs and perform the old dances. They share traditional arts and crafts and recipes. They play games and march in parades. It's a time to celebrate what it means to be Arapaho.

A group of Arapaho proudly march in a parade in Gallup, New Mexico.

To Find Out More

Here are some additional resources to help you learn more about the Arapaho:

 **Books**

Gibson, Karen Bush. **The Arapaho: Hunters of the Great Plains.** Bridgestone Books, 2003.

Korman, Susan. **Horse Raid: An Arapaho Camp in the 1800s.** Soundprints, 1998.

Lassieur, Allison. **The Arapaho Tribe.** Capstone Press, 2002.

Miller, Jay. **American Indian Families.** Children's Press, 1996.

Miller, Jay. **American Indian Festivals.** Children's Press, 1996.

Organizations and Online Sites

The Arapaho Project
http://www.colorado.edu/ csilw/arapahoproject/

Visit this site to learn more about the Arapaho language and culture.

National Museum of the American Indian
Fourth Street and Independence Avenue SW Washington, DC 20024 202-633-1000 *http://www.nmai.si.edu/*

Visit the museum to learn more about American Indians.

Nihancan and the Dwarf's Arrow
http://www.indigenouspeople. net/nihancan.htm

Read a traditional Arapaho story.

Northern Arapaho Tribe
www.northernarapaho.com

Learn more about the Northern Arapaho and their reservation.

Important Words

complex having many steps or parts

culture the way of life of a group of people

famine an extreme lack of food

linguistic anthropologist a scientist who studies language and culture

migrate moving from one region to another

negotiate discussing a situation to solve problems or reach an agreement

nomadic moving from place to place

ritual action that is always performed in the same way as part of a religious ceremony or other celebration

sacred holy; having to do with religion; something deserving of great respect

settlers people who move into an area and build homes there

Index

Meet the Author

Christin Ditchfield is an author, conference speaker, and host of the nationally syndicated radio program *Take It to Heart!* Her articles have been featured in magazines all over the world. A former elementary school teacher, Christin has written more than thirty books for children on a wide range of topics, including sports, science, and history. She makes her home in Sarasota, Florida.